To **Kalluk**, my beloved bossy boots Alaskan Malamute packmate, and his pals **Toshi**, **Kai** and **Piff**.
And in memory of **Herman**, who was the best.

Animal Welfare Institute
900 Pennsylvania Avenue, SE
Washington, DC 20003
www.awionline.org

Copyright © 2008 Sheila Hamanaka
ISBN: 978-0-938414-91-9
LCN: 2008940651
Printed in the United States

Written and Illustrated by:
Sheila Hamanaka

Design by:
Ava Rinehart and
Cameron Creinin

Pablo Puppy's Search for the Perfect Person

Animal Welfare Institute

ANIMAL
SHELTER

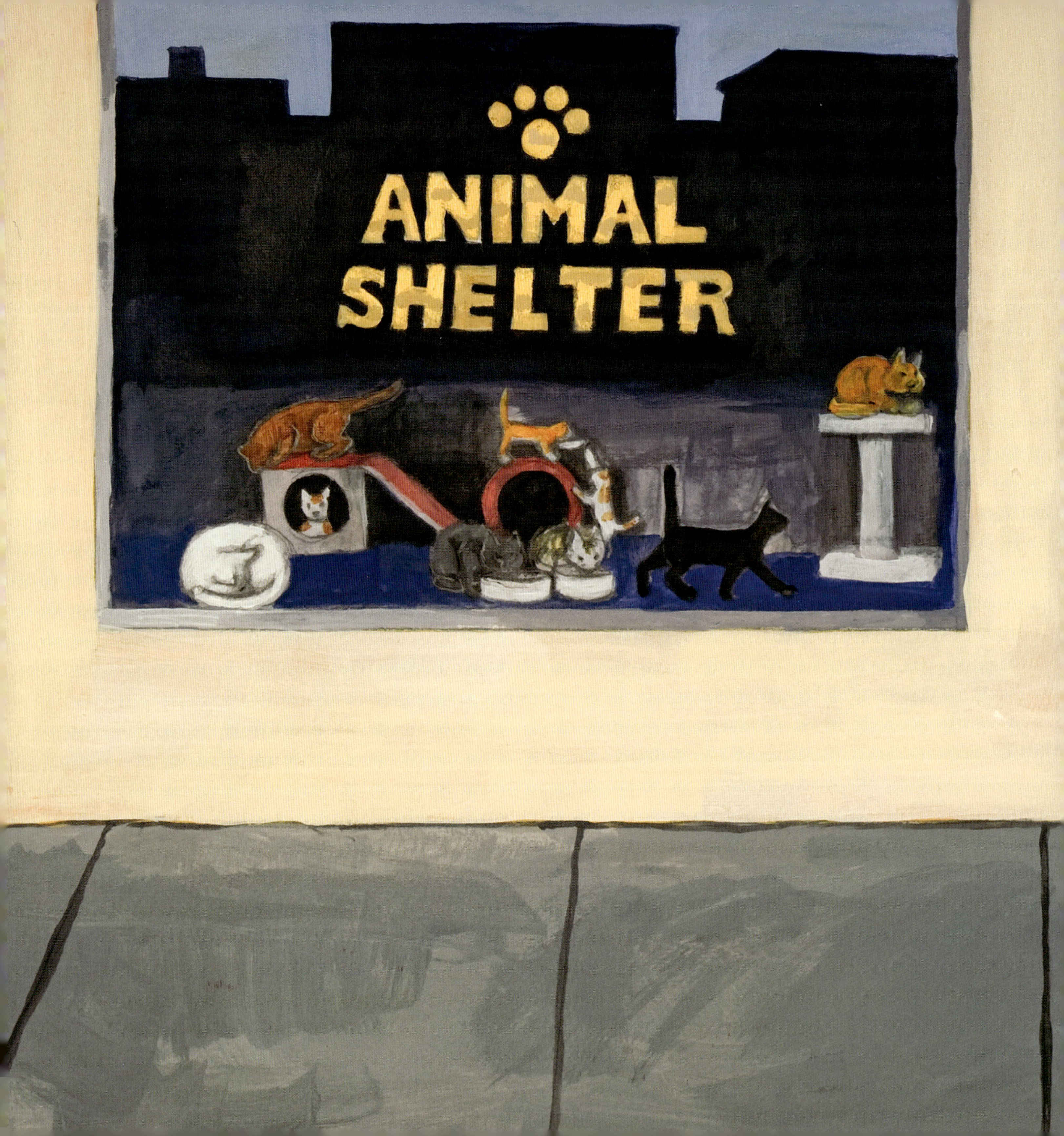

Pablo was lucky.

He was a homeless puppy, but a kind person took him to an animal shelter.

It was full of cats and dogs who had no home.

Pablo was nervous. A man dressed in green put him in a kennel.

There, Pablo met Natasha. She was big and old. And very sad.

"Why are you sad?" asked Pablo, who was happy to find a friend.

Finding a friend is like finding a pot of gold.

"Lots of people come here
to find a dog friend," she
said. "But many of them
want a cute little puppy.
Natasha sighed.

Nobody wants an old dog like me.

And if you make one mistake, some people will throw you away."
"That's not very nice," said Pablo.
"Well, I hope you find a perfect person," said Natasha. *I will*, thought Pablo...

I know I will...

"Um, what does a perfect person look like?" asked Pablo.

"Perfect people come in all colors," said Natasha.

"Some are young and some are old. Some walk fast and some walk slowly. Some carry canes and some roll around in chairs with big wheels.

Perfect people make sure their **dog friends** get exercise."

"What's exercise?" asked Pablo. "Is it something to eat?"

"Oh, no," said Natasha. "It's long walks and toys that are tossed.

Perfect people **love to play.** That's why perfect people are often children."

"And what does the **perfect** person sound like?" asked Pablo.

"A perfect person knows a dog has excellent hearing, so perfect people never **shout**. And they will never, ever hit you," said Natasha.

"Some speak to you in English.
Some speak to you in Spanish,
or Chinese, or Swahili, or hundreds
of other languages."

"Do people speak **dog**?"
asked Pablo.

"Perfect people know that dogs speak
with their whole bodies," said Natasha.

Pablo's stomach started to growl.

"I think your tummy is talking to us," said Natasha.

"I'm hungry," said Pablo.

"Ah, food," said Natasha.

"A perfect person will feed a puppy like you four times a day."

"Four times? " asked Pablo.

"That's Perfect!

And what about when I grow up?"

"Two times a day," replied Natasha.

"It's best to stay trim."

"What about water?" Pablo asked.

"A perfect person will give you a separate bowl of perfectly clean water, fresh every day!" Natasha told him.

"And puppies get lots of safe toys to chew on, and lots of **treats**.

Perfect people use treats to reward you for good manners."

Pablo was getting sleepy,
and he snuggled next to Natasha.
"Tell me more," he said yawning.
"A perfect person gives you a bed.
An old, folded
blanket will do...
...but sometimes beds are fancy!"
Something tiny
jumped off of Pablo.
A flea!

"That reminds me," said Natasha. "A perfect person will brush you everyday. And sometimes they will give you a bath."

Pablo was amazed. "A perfect person has a lot to do," he said. "Why would they do it?"

"Because they are kind," said Natasha, "and full of love."

"Love?" asked Pablo.

He wasn't sure what it was,
but he thought he loved Natasha.
She was so kind to him.

"Yes, love," said Natasha. "Love means taking a puppy out many times a day, even in the rain."

"Or the snow?" He asked.

"Yes," said Natasha. "A perfect person will take a puppy outside right after the puppy wakes up, or eats, or finishes playing. And every time a puppy goes potty outside, a perfect person gives the puppy a treat!"

"What if I have an accident?" asked Pablo.

"Don't worry," said Natasha. "A perfect person will never yell at you or hit you if you make a mistake."

"That's good," said Pablo. "I get scared when people yell."

"A perfect person knows that no one is really perfect," said Natasha.

The dogs in the shelter began to bark.

People were coming!

Pablo hid between Natasha's legs and peeked out.

Would he find the **perfect** person?

"Look at that cute puppy!" said a woman.
"He's too small!" replied the man
in a ***loud*** voice.
They kept walking.

Next came a boy and his mother.

"Look at that cute puppy!" exclaimed the boy.

"Oh, no!" said the mother. "If a puppy had an accident on my new rug, I would scream."

Natasha was glad when they walked away.

She liked Pablo and didn't want him to leave.

Next came a little girl and her grandmother.

"Look at that cute puppy!" the little girl said.

"Puppies are a lot of work," said the grandmother.

"Will you feed him four times a day?"

"Yes!" said the girl.

"And will you brush him every day?"

"Yes!" said the girl.

"And will you take him outside to go potty many times a day, even in the rain?" asked the grandmother.

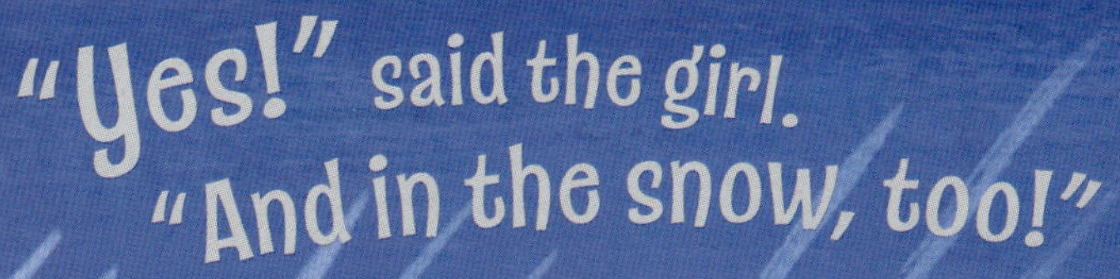

"Yes!" said the girl.
"And in the snow, too!"

The grandmother looked deep into the girl's eyes.

"And most important of all," she said, "do you promise *never* to yell at the puppy or to hit him, even if he makes a mistake?"

"Yes!" said the girl, who was very wise.

She knew that all puppies make mistakes—just like children do.

"Of course, it will cost money to take the puppy to the veterinarian for checkups," said the grandmother.

"I will make cookies and sell them at a bake sale to help out," said the girl.

"Perfect!" said the grandmother.

Pablo was excited!
He had found the perfect person!
The man in green took Pablo
out of the kennel so he could
meet the girl.
He wagged his tail and
licked her hand.

Pablo looked back at Natasha.
She looked very, very sad.
Suddenly Pablo understood why.
He was going to have to leave Natasha!

Then the girl said, "The puppy's friend looks very sad."
"Yes," said the grandmother. "Dogs have feelings too. She is going to miss her friend."
"Grandma,"
said the little girl,
"can we..."

"Well," said the grandmother, thinking it over.

She knew that adopting a dog was a big decision, because a dog friend is a friend forever.

"Yes! I need a friend who will take long, slow walks with me.

I think I have found the perfect dog!"

About the Animal Welfare Institute

The Animal Welfare Institute (AWI) was founded in 1951 to reduce the pain and fear people cause animals. AWI helps a wide range of animals in need, including those used in experimental laboratories, confined on factory farms, caught in steel traps in the woods, and threatened with extinction across the globe—from the smallest mice to the great whales of the sea. We believe that each person can make a difference for the animals by stepping up to help those who are suffering or are in need of a little assistance. Why don't you join us in making the world a better place for all? For more information, please visit AWI at:

www.awionline.org

About the Author-Illustrator

Sheila Hamanaka is an award-winning children's book author-illustrator whose work focuses on multiculturalism and peace. Her books include the popular *All the Colors of the Earth; The Journey: Japanese Americans, Racism, and Renewal; Grandparent's Song*; and *Be-Bop-A-Do-Walk.* Deeply concerned about our fellow animals and the future of our planet, Hamanaka wrote and illustrated three other books for the Animal Welfare Institute: *The Boy Who Loved All Living Things: The Imaginary Childhood Journal of Albert Schweitzer* (2006); *Kamie Cat's Terrible Night* (2010); and, *A Dangerous Life* (2014), a graphic novel about saving elephants.

Download free Pablo Puppy and Kamie Cat activities for children from the Animal Welfare Institute website: www.awionline.org/educationalmaterials